TO TERESA.

Tom McNay

Advance praise for Don McNay and *The Unbridled World of Ernie Fletcher*

"Thank goodness there are still journalists like Don McNay left in Kentucky and America: fearless, truthful, compelling, and willing to take on powerful interests. He's what the First Amendment was all about two centuries back. Do yourself a favor, and buy this book."

- John Eckberg, author of *Road Dog*; *The Success Effect*; and a business reporter at *The Cincinnati Enquirer*

"Don McNay came to journalism relatively late, but he quickly proved that he has some attributes of fine journalists--a nose for news, a sense of justice, a capacity for outrage about injustice, a sympathy for the average person, a willingness to speak truth to power, and a sense of humor."

- Al Cross, Director of the Institute for Rural Journalism and Community Issues, based at the University of Kentucky, and political writer for *The Courier-Journal* for 15 1/2 years

"The claimed accomplishments of a political leader can only be measured with good and accurate information, and the consistent reports of Don McNay certainly provide that reliable news."

- Julian M. Carroll , Kentucky State Senator and Former Kentucky Governor

"Rock 'n' roll can parallel life and politics in ways that are funny, ironic, incisive and profound, and thus, Don McNay engages his readers. Lyrics from the likes of John Mellencamp and Melissa Etheridge spotlight McNay's tough topics, and McNay's research and plainspoken style enlightens."

- Suzette Martinez Standring, Immediate Past President, National Society of Newspaper Columnists

"In rapid time, Don McNay has emerged as a powerful voice for disempowered Kentuckians: men and women who work hard and play by the rules, but whose quest for a share of the American Dream is frustrated by corrupt politicians and special interests. May his voice continue to resonate."

- Jonathan Miller, Kentucky State Treasurer and author of *The Compassionate Community: Ten Values to Unite America*

"Thank God the SOB wasn't writing back when I ran for office."

- Rick Robinson, Fort Mitchell attorney, former congressional aide, and former congressional candidate

"It is rare that a political columnist can demand accountability from public figures in a manner that is neither mean-spirited nor disrespectful. Don McNay has remarkable insight into the actual people behind the public figure, and his musings balance the personal success and failures we all face. He writes with humor and compassion about issues that affect all Kentuckians."

- Joni Jenkins, State Representative, Kentucky 44th District; Chair, Jefferson County Legislative Delegation and Vice Chair, Kentucky Democratic Party

"Some people like to go to the track and catch a race or to the stadium and watch nine innings. They go with a pencil behind their ear--and they keep notes. They may curse the stumbling horse or the third baseman's sloppy glove. But they curse them out of love, as a mother scolds a wayward child. Don McNay may love horses, he may love baseball. I honestly don't know. But I do know he loves politics, and he keeps notes. Like any true fan, his aspersions are from the heart. He only wants that horse to run like he did in the morning workout, that third baseman to catch like he did in the minors, and that governor to govern the way he promised to in the campaign."

- Mark Neikirk, Managing Editor of the *Cincinnati Post* and the *Kentucky Post*

"Don McNay's snappy writing is an always-too-brief joy to read, as he exercises his sharp wit on the proud and powerful, giving a practical and down-to-earth take on how political maneuverings and economic rumblings affect regular Kentuckians."

- Jim Gaines, Political Reporter for the *Bowling Green Daily News*

"Don McNay knows Kentucky and isn't afraid to call 'em as he sees 'em--and have a good laugh at 'em as well."

- Samantha Bennett, Columnist for the *Pittsburgh Post-Gazette* and Vice President of the National Society of Newspaper Columnists

"Don McNay is a keen observer of today's political, social, and economic landscape. He writes colorfully, clearly, and with great humor. But more than that, he exhibits the courage to speak the truth no matter the consequences. Such courage is a rare commodity in today's world."

- Bill Garmer, Lexington Trial Attorney, Association of Trial Lawyers of America Governor and Former Chair of the Kentucky Democratic Party

"Don McNay is one of those fearless folks we all want to be. His writing is both wittingly disarming and courageously straightforward. McNay speaks and writes in a language we can all understand and never pulls punches. Taking on the establishment is easy; doing it with charm, style, and clarity of reasoned thought makes for a very good read."

- Alan Stein, President, Lexington Legends Professional Baseball Team

The Unbridled World Of Ernie Fletcher

Reflections on Kentucky's Governor

by
Don McNay

Bloomington, IN Milton Keynes, UK

authorHOUSE®

AuthorHouse™
1663 Liberty Drive, Suite 200
Bloomington, IN 47403
www.authorhouse.com
Phone: 1-800-839-8640

AuthorHouse™ UK Ltd.
500 Avebury Boulevard
Central Milton Keynes, MK9 2BE
www.authorhouse.co.uk
Phone: 08001974150

First published by AuthorHouse 9/11/2006

ISBN: 1-4259-6244-0 (sc)
ISBN: 1-4259-6245-9 (dj)

Library of Congress Control Number: 2006908210

Printed in the United States of America
Bloomington, Indiana

This book is printed on acid-free paper.

Photo on the front cover courtesy of Nancy Taggart and the Richmond Register.

To Joe and Ollie McNay, who were my past.

To: Abijah, Angela, Gena, Clay, Nick, Lyndsay, Theresa and Lynn, who are my present and future.

And to those four people who provided the margin in Ernie Fletcher's win over Mark Metcalf in the 1996, 6ᵗʰ district of Kentucky, Republican, congressional primary. You know who you are. Without you, this book would have never been written.

Contents

Introduction

You may ask yourself, 'How did I get here?'
- Talking Heads

I'm sure Governor Ernie Fletcher sometimes asks himself the question: How did I wind up being governor of Kentucky?

The only consistent thing about Governor Fletcher's career path is that there has been no consistency. He was a doctor, a fighter pilot, a minister, a state representative, and a congressman before he was elected governor.

Unlike several former governors, who dreamt of the office since grade school, Fletcher came into politics from a nonpolitical background. Lack of experience has accounted for a number of his problems.

He came in with the message of "cleaning up the mess in Frankfort" and promptly got into a mess himself.

Fletcher's move into the Governor's Mansion coincided with my return as a columnist. I had written a community column for the *Lexington Herald-Leader* in the early 1980's but had since stopped writing for 20 years.

One of life's great ironies occurred shortly after Fletcher's inauguration.

Jodi Whitaker, news editor at the *Richmond Register*, asked if
I wanted to write a column for their business page. Jodi left
the *Register* a few months later to go into state government and
eventually wound up as Governor Fletcher's press secretary.

She became Fletcher's press secretary at the same time that I
became a press secretary's worst nightmare.

Like Dan Quayle did for David Letterman or Bill Clinton did for
Jay Leno, Fletcher has given me lot of opportunity to poke fun—an
opportunity which I have taken.

You can read about it in the following chapters. I poke, yell, prod,
and suggest other perspectives for the Governor to look at.

I give Fletcher credit when credit is due, like with his initiative
to have broadband access in every part of the state. I also
acknowledge his diligence in trying to improve Medicaid. He may
eventually stop Kentuckians for paying for the $2000 aspirins I
write about in this book.

Until he was indicted, I consistently thought that he would be re-
elected. He still could be.

Re-election would give me four more years of things to write
about. I couldn't imagine another governor buzzing the United
States Capitol in an airplane, building a secret door to their office,
or driving a limo the 500 feet between their office and home.

A new governor would take away my best material. I would have
to drop the "Unbridled" theme, a trademark for me. Millions
of dollars will go down the drain as "Unbridled" has become
completely identified with Ernie Fletcher.

The book is broken up into two parts. The first part is about
Governor Fletcher and his supporting cast. The second part is

about the issues that Kentucky ought to be talking about instead of noodling, etiquette, logos, and limo rides.

It is not a biography, but rather, it sheds a different light on the question of how Governor Fletcher got to where he is today.

PART I

The Unbridled Governor
and His Supporting Cast

www.
DonMcNay
.com

Unbridled Penguin

"I've been a puppet, a pauper, a pirate, a poet, a pawn and a king"
- Frank Sinatra

Like Frank Sinatra, Governor Ernie Fletcher has had his ups and downs, but I thought 2005 would be an up year for him. That was before I heard about the $645,075 bill for the state logo.

The governor, like those who max out their credit cards during the holidays, kicked off the New Year with an unexpected debt.

Governor Fletcher has been a doctor, preacher and fighter pilot. None of those careers provide training for negotiating business deals.

Over a five month period, an advertising firm billed the state $645,075 for coming up with the new state logo, "Unbridled Spirit." It consists of the word "Kentucky" with a horse's head sketched at the end.

During that same five months, my family helped me develop a new logo for my website, www.donmcnay.com. The bill will be less than $100.

Fletcher's logo has a horse, and mine has a penguin in sunglasses playing the drums. Other than that, I can't tell much difference.

It could not cost $645,000 to have a horse pose for you. There are more horses in Kentucky than drum-playing penguins. The governor made a bad deal.

The advertising company's bill averaged $129,015 per month, and the bill is ongoing.

My bill stopped once I got my penguin. I am way ahead of the governor on that issue.

If the governor had asked me to come up with a logo for him, I could have gathered the right crew for less than $645,075.

If someone had tried to explain that the state could use $645,075 to help children or improve healthcare, it probably would not have gotten the governor's attention.

Yet I'll bet if he would have seen how $645,075 could be used for things that are REALLY important to him, he might have been interested in working out a different deal.

The governor hired his sister-in-law for a $25,000 a year job. With $645,075, he could have put 25 more relatives on the payroll or made a nice down payment on a decent state airplane.

$129,015 a month would pay the salary of 10 staff members that are now earning $125,000 a year. Better yet, he could hire 144 minimum-wage park workers to replace all of those he fired for having long hair, tattoos and their shirttails out.

Fletcher spent $5,871 for a secret door in the capitol to duck from reporters. $645,071 could have gotten him 109 secret doors installed. He could have even had an entourage like Elvis and spent the $129,000 a month on flunkies to beat up those pesky media types.

I know Fletcher would have liked that more than any bumper sticker.

I want to negotiate a deal with Governor Fletcher. Rather than the state coughing up $129,015 a month, I will work for about $100,000 a month instead.

The state will save money, and I will throw in some items that the governor would really like.

My daughter, who drew the penguin, can also draw a horse, which may or may not wear sunglasses. She would make sure the horse did not have long hair, tattoos or a shirttail hanging out.

For $100,000 a month, I would put some of his relatives on my payroll and install secret doors all over my office. I would let him use them anytime he wanted. I do not have a plane, but I can give him some discount airline coupons that I have been holding onto.

I know lots of reporters and could hire one to be beaten up every month. I have five cats and a dog that would serve as an excellent entourage, and for $100,000 a month, I would even hang out with the governor myself. Frank Sinatra liked his entourage to wear tuxes; I could wear mine if I lose a little weight.

Like Frank Sinatra, Governor Fletcher has had his ups and downs in life. Sticking the state with a $645,075 bill for a bumper sticker was not one of his up moments.

Especially since he could have gotten a drum-playing penguin for $100.

Unbridled Space Aliens

"I'm not the man they think I am at home.
I'm a Rocket Man"
- Elton John (also performed by William Shatner)

Governor Fletcher can sometimes appear to be like a character in *National Lampoon's Vacation*. Every time he leaves town, something terrible happens.

He caused the U.S. Capitol to be evacuated when he flew to President Bush's re-inauguration. He left to tour Europe while the state teachers marched to keep their health insurance from being cut.

While he is traveling in Asia, the state Bureau of Investigation slapped subpoenas on his office, employees, political cronies and business partners.

Fletcher's being gone during a crisis did not make sense to me until I got an email from my old friend Rob Dollar.

Rob is organizing the Hopkinsville Little Green Man Festival from August 19 to 21.

It turns out that Western Kentucky had a visit from 12 little green men in a flying saucer fifty years ago. The incident happened outside of Hopkinsville in a small town called Kelly, but it sounds like visitors from space know their way around Kentucky.

Suddenly, things make sense. Governor Fletcher's botched trips are part of a larger mission. He is secretly working to recruit space aliens back to Kentucky.

Space aliens could help him in a lot of ways. Governor Fletcher has received a lot of criticism for the way his Department of Transportation is being run. He's had problems with road contractors charging the state too much. Also, the department has fired good people and let political cronies take their places.

There are no highways in space. If Fletcher develops a way for Kentuckians to travel by flying saucer, he can help himself politically and save the state a ton of money.

I'm starting to think that Fletcher is subtly reaching out to space aliens. An example would be the Transportation Cabinet's record on minority hiring.

The Federal Highway Administration is ready to crack down on Kentucky and possibly cut off millions of dollars because their hiring record is so bad.

Out of the 317 people hired by the Transportation Department, 310 were white people. Only seven were minorities and none of the seven are in high positions.

It appears from the outside to be blatant racism, but Fletcher could have a bigger plan.

There were only seven Mercury Astronauts that started the American space program. By only hiring seven minority workers, it might be a secret message of some kind to the space aliens.

He won't need the millions of federal highway dollars if he gets the state converted to flying saucers, and he might try to argue that all humans are a minority in outer space.

Making a pitch to aliens would also explain what happened on the way to the presidential inauguration.

In almost every movie about aliens, there is a scene where a flying saucer approaches Washington and people start to scurry everywhere.

Although it happens in the movies, it never happened in real life until Governor Fletcher scared most of Washington.

It was a way to show the little green men that he could connect at their level.

A deal with the aliens would be good for Fletcher. He could ship the merit employees off to another planet and replace them with friends of his cronies and relatives of his business partners.

If he doesn't get re-elected as governor, he could make a fortune as a speaker at UFO and Star Trek conventions. He could pump that money into more condo deals in Florida.

Thus, don't be surprised that if the Little Green Men come back to Hopkinsville this August, they will be greeted by Governor Ernie Fletcher. The aliens will look at Fletcher and say, "Take us to your leader."

Governor Fletcher will then introduce them to Senator Mitch McConnell.

Governor Fletcher's Unbridled Limo Ride

"The trail is long, and the river is wide.
And my ride's here."
- Warren Zevon

The trail from the Kentucky Governor's office to the Governor's mansion is about 500 feet. There is a not a river, swamp, nor alligator between them.

I'm 100 pounds heavier than Governor Ernie Fletcher, and I can walk it.

Fletcher has a Lincoln Town Car drive him from spot to spot.

The waste of taxpayers' money is something to get mad about. At $3 per gallon, it is costing a bundle to have a state trooper drive Fletcher 500 feet.

I'd rather he spend tax dollars on something like the $5000 secret door to his office.

The secret door will be there when the next governor takes over. Wasted fuel won't be.

It is a horrible symbol that the governor is too lazy to walk 500 feet.

I partially empathize with what Fletcher is doing. I used to live a block from my office and occasionally drove. I felt like a fool firing up the car and going around the block but did it anyway.

There have been mornings when I've looked like I had been on a three-day bender (I have never been on a three-day bender, but I have the look perfected) and did not want to interact with neighbors. When I was walking to work, I had to.

With his troopers, car, and secret door, the governor never has to interact with someone who is not on his payroll.

Maybe that is why his popularity is at 28%. Meeting a few "regular folks" might give him an idea of what people are thinking about.

Dan Rather wrote *The Palace Guard* about President Nixon and said that a lot of Nixon's problems stemmed from his being isolated from the public. It might be a good idea for Fletcher to thumb through a copy of that book.

If he takes it to heart, it might save the state a few gallons of gas.

It's not the gas I am really upset about. Every governor wastes money, and Fletcher is no exception.Yet governors are still supposed to set an example for the rest of the state to follow.

It's hard for a fat guy like me to be inspired when my governor takes a 500-foot limo ride.

Fletcher threw away the one issue that might have spurred a political comeback for him. The limo story is getting national coverage, and people will be laughing at Kentucky once more.

It won't get as many chuckles as when he buzzed the United States Capitol in an airplane, but it is still a knee-slapper.

Governor Fletcher is a former minister and doctor, and he has the perfect credentials to preach the gospel of healthy living. He could talk to Kentuckians in a doctor-to-patient manner.

Every time I go to my doctor, he tells me to start exercising. He never mentions taking a ride in a limo.

Although my weight recently went from grossly obese to just obese, I am a better spokesperson for fitness than the governor is.

Two years ago, I started a group called Don's Fat Guys in Richmond. We meet each week and inspire each other to lose weight.

We recently changed our name to Don's Get-Fit Guys. Many in the group are no longer fat, and getting fit is our goal.

We ought to invite the governor to join our meetings. We can explain why riding 500 feet is bad behavior.

Warren Zevon's song, "My Ride's Here," is about the kind of vehicle the grim reaper might have.

Fletcher needs to set an example for all of Kentucky. He also needs to realize that in a high-stress job such as governor, walking and exercising is a way to ensure that he doesn't go on that ride earlier than he should.

Unbridled Noodling

"You dropped a bomb on me."
- **Gap Band**

A bomb was dropped on Kentucky Governor Ernie Fletcher when he was indicted on three misdemeanor counts. Until the recent indictments, I steadfastly believed that he would be re-elected. I do not think so now.

The governor keeps trying to trivialize the investigation and compare it to a law violation against noodling (hand-fishing); however, any indictment, even for noodling, is not going to help you politically.

The great criminal lawyer Frank Haddad said, "No one ever looks good in a mug shot."

No one ever looks good being indicted either.

I do not know if the governor listens to fellow Republican Larry Forgy. Fletcher has a knack for listening to bad advisors, and Forgy fits that description. Forgy has never held public office despite many efforts but loves to be in the public eye.

Forgy has been espousing a "bounce-back" theory. Forgy is convinced that the public will be outraged over the indictments and that Fletcher will jump up in the polls.

Theories like "bounce-back" might explain why Forgy could never get elected to anything. He is disconnected from reality.

Ask O.J. Simpson or Michael Jackson if being indicted helped their careers. I do not see them doing Hertz and Pepsi commercials anymore. They spend most of their time dodging creditors.

O.J. and Michael were two of the most popular people in America. Neither one has "bounced back" and won't.

Fletcher has the same public approval problem.

I would like to think that people can distinguish between being indicted and being found guilty, but most people cannot. Many people assume that grand juries only indict people who have done something wrong.

Since approximately 90% of those indicted get convicted, Fletcher is up against tough odds.

There are two ways to bounce back politically--outrage and forgiveness. Fletcher keeps hoping for outrage. I wish him luck.

People will get outraged if they think that someone has been unjustly sentenced for a serious crime. Since the governor compared the merit system investigation to noodling, no one is going to care if he goes down for it, especially since he pardoned anyone who might roll over on him.

Handing out pardons like Halloween candy made people think that Fletcher had something to hide. A "not guilty" verdict will not erase that perception.

Forgiveness works but only after the accused steps up and accepts punishment.

Both Martha Stewart and Michael Milken have legitimate complaints about being unfairly prosecuted. Both went to jail for "crimes" that no one else has ever served time for.

Both fought the law and then sucked it up and took their punishment. Both are now more popular than ever.

Americans like it when people say, "I'm sorry." They don't like it when you whine.

If Fletcher has any plans to stay in politics, he had better figure that out.

A governor, now indicted, who came into office with the theme of cleaning up "waste, fraud and abuse", is in an impossible spot.

I wonder if Fletcher will be more empathic toward people seeking pardons or having their death sentence commuted. In *The Bonfire of Vanities*, Tom Wolfe wrote, "A liberal is a conservative who has been arrested."

That would also have to extend to being indicted.

If Fletcher is sincerely outraged about being indicted, he should maybe try examining how well the judicial system works for all Kentuckians. If he feels like the system is unfair to wealthy politicians with high-powered lawyers, he might do well to consider how difficult it is for the poor and disadvantaged to fight for justice.

If Fletcher examines whether the judicial system is fair to all people, he might score some "bounce-back" points. If he wants to act like he is the only person indicted that is not happy about it, he is not going to win anyone over.

Fletcher is accused of crimes that have potential fines and jail time, which may require the forfeiture of public office and the loss of his medical license.   Everything he worked for could be taken away.

If I had a bomb like that fall on me, I would not compare it to noodling.

Unbridled Etiquette

"Don't you know about the new fashion, honey?
All you need are looks and a whole lotta money."
- Billy Joel

Mark Hebert at WHAS TV in Louisville did a story about
the Kentucky Labor Cabinet hiring a consultant to teach their
employees proper manners.

The employees were told they needed to bathe daily and wear real
gold and silver instead of the fake stuff.

The consultant said that "conservative dress was a symbol of
conservative political beliefs."

The story made me angry. I'm still mad about the state firing
park workers with long hair and tattoos. I thought this was another
example of Fletcher's team treating state employees like servants at
their country clubs.

Then I realized the problem. The consultant did not understand the
techniques necessary to work in state government.

Instead of telling employees to take a bath, she needed to be
teaching the things that they really need to know.

For example, there is a proper way to greet a government contractor. A state employee needs to use phrases like "money is no object" and "your wish is my command" in the presence of any contractor who contributed to the governor's campaign.

Otherwise, the employees will find themselves fired or transferred to Paducah. Proper manners can save a state employee's career.

The governor's political staff needs to follow a different code when dealing with contractors. They should extend the right hand for a firm handshake and keep the left jacket pocket exposed so that the contractor can stuff a wad of checks in it.

A political staffer should always wear a suit or jacket. Preferably one with big pockets.

Many people have seen guests who will not leave a party at the proper ending time. The manners consultant may have addressed that situation in her training.

State supervisors need to know how to ask people to leave state government jobs so that the governor's friends can take their places.

The term for a person staying late at a party is called a "straggler." The term for someone trying to keep a merit job is called a "Democrat."

There is a proper way to deal with both.

With a "straggler" you should walk the guest to the door and hope they politely leave.

With a "Democrat" you should transfer them to a job far from their homes and hope they politely retire.

I'm not sure whether or not the manners consultant discussed written communications. A handwritten note is an important social tool, but email is gauche.

There is a penalty called the "indictment" for those in state government who make this social faux pas.

An indictment is almost as serious as not being listed on the social register.

Holding a door open is a part of good manners. Governor Fletcher showed his mastery of etiquette by putting in a secret door to his office. The $5000 door was seen as a waste of taxpayers' money, but it was actually the first step in helping the governor follow proper social procedures.

Instead of encountering an ill-mannered reporter, who may or may not have bathed, the governor can avoid contact with that ilk.

It would probably be a good idea to add a secret door to the Franklin County courthouse so that the governor's staff can avoid reporters as indictments are handed down.

Bad manners breed bad manners, and the governor's staff does not want to fall to the level of reporters.

Especially since few reporters wear a Rolex.

If any of the governor's appointees are convicted of a crime, it will send all their manners training right out the window.

The consultant for the Labor Cabinet said that conservative dress is equated with conservative thought.

Bright orange prison jump suits send the wrong fashion message. People will think they are radical, liberal Democrats.

Being seen as a Democrat would be harder on the Fletcher people than a stay in the big house.

They won't be able to flash real gold and silver in jail, and I am not sure if daily bathing is part of the routine.

If Fletcher's staff people get convicted, they will have to add a special new etiquette program—one on maintaining good manners while making "Unbridled Spirit" license plates.

Unbridled Jerry Springer Imitator

"I didn't know I'd find her on daytime TV.
My whole world lays waiting behind door number three."
- Jimmy Buffett and Steve Goodman

The Jerry Springer show is one of many strange things you see on daytime television.

Yet Jerry Springer did not set out to be the Jerry Springer that we know and hate.

Springer was the Mayor of Cincinnati when I was growing up. Even after being caught paying a hooker with a check, Springer still won the election.

Not many guys overcome a stunt like that, but Springer had tremendous intellect and moxy. When he left politics, he took his charisma into broadcasting and became a serious news anchor. Springer went national with the idea of doing an intelligent talk show.

It did not work. Springer was dying in the ratings, so he changed his format.

He filled every episode with strange topics and invited every weirdo loser in America to be on the show. Now, appearing on

Jerry Springer's show is an indication that you are completely crazy.

Governor Fletcher must be sitting behind his $5,000 secret door watching the Springer show.

Fletcher had a bad year—a really bad year. He came into office with the theme of cleaning up waste, fraud, and abuse. I do not think he is going to stick with that much longer.

In developing a backup plan, it looks like he took some cues from Jerry Springer himself. Instead of focusing on issues that really matter, he is looking to get people angry and throwing chairs at one other.

In an effort to boost his opinion poll ratings, Fletcher is harping on the most polarizing and divisive issues he can come up with. It worked for Springer, and it might work for Fletcher too.

Jobs and pensions are disappearing while healthcare costs keep going up. Medicaid needs to be fixed, and schools need to be improved. We need better roads and airports to attract high-paying jobs.

Instead of dealing with those problems, Fletcher decided that we need to focus on busting up unions and taking away the rights of injury victims. Lt. Governor Steve Pence has chimed in suggesting that we need chemical castrations for sex offenders.

Castration will always get more attention than policy discussions.

I think Fletcher is on to something. More people buy *The National Enquirer* than *U.S. News and World Report*.

Many television news stations have dropped political coverage and instead, focus on sex, drugs, and gore.

There is a cynical view that suggests that people do not want to hear about serious problems and that the media really does not want to cover them.

It could also be that Fletcher is setting himself up to follow Springer into television.

By researching all the hot-button issues, Fletcher will have a leg up when he makes his move.

I can see Fletcher starring in a few different shows right now.

In the Fletcher version of *The Apprentice*, when Fletcher says, "You're fired," Republican Party Chair Daryl Brock replies, "Forget about it."

On *Law and Order, Special Governor's Unit*, Fletcher would pardon everybody, every week, no matter what they had done. Even before they do it.

In the Fletcher version of *That 70's Show*, Ernie would drag out examples of past governors from the 1970's or maybe even the 1870's and explain how his mistakes weren't as bad as theirs.

A real hit would be to revive *Lets Make a Deal*, and let Fletcher replace Monty Hall as host. Fletcher's cronies could have their idiot relatives dress up in silly outfits and answer questions.

If they got the answers wrong, Fletcher would give them a state job anyway.

Ernie would be a natural for the part where a contestant chooses whatever is behind a secret door.

Behind one door would be a ride to Washington in the state airplane. Door number two would be tickets to the next Mitch

McConnell fundraiser. Behind door number three would be Fletcher himself, ready to hand out a pardon.

Depending on what the contestant needed, their whole world could lie waiting behind door number three.

Unbridled Penguin Hunting

"Oh Lord, won't you buy me a Mercedes Benz? My friends all drive Porsches, I must made amends."
- Janis Joplin

I almost feel sorry for Jim Host. The secretary of the Kentucky Commerce Cabinet was the subject of my weekly column more than any state official.

Host is to me what Michael Jackson was to Jay Leno. I am sure that Leno doesn't really want to always tell jokes about Jackson, but Jackson's lifestyle keeps giving Leno good material.

I'm that way with Host.

First, his Parks Department made the stupid decision to fire park workers who had long hair, earrings, tattoos and shirttails. Then, he got the state to spend hundreds of thousands of dollars on our snazzy state logo, "Unbridled Spirit."

I was able to obtain my logo, a rock and roll penguin, for $100. His group spent big money to "design" a logo that is almost identical to the logo for the Denver Broncos football team.

No football team has a logo that resembles a rock and roll penguin. I have it all over Host on that one.

Host and State Auditor Crit Luallen hosted a fundraiser to help the University of Kentucky's Rural Journalism program, which was ironic, since Host and Luallen were fighting at the time.

I guess they still are. In his ongoing quest to find, "waste, fraud and abuse," Host was critical of an audit that Luallan's staff did of the Commerce Cabinet. He told her she needed to look harder to find someone who was taking advantage of the state.

Luallan went back and found a man who was using his state credit card for personal items: Jim Host.

Host used his credit card for $95.49 worth of camping equipment and charged $46.61 to print pictures of Governor Fletcher's "Spring Turkey Hunt".

Host is a wealthy man and can afford to buy his own camping equipment. Even if he were not rich, taxpayers should not be paying for guys to go camping with the governor.

Spring is here, and Host may decide to change the hunt into the "Spring Penguin Hunt," and send the hunters after me.

Since he is trying hard to use the state logo, they will probably call it the "Unbridled Penguin Hunt."

Host did not apologize for buying the camping equipment. He did not see any problem since he turned the equipment over to the Fish and Wildlife Department after he was finished with it.

Host seems to think that he can have the state buy him new stuff, as long as he turns it over to a state agency later.

I want Jim to cut me in on the same deal.

I'd like for the state to buy me a new Mercedes Benz. I'll make sure to turn it over to a state agency once I have driven it for a year or so.

If Host could throw in a state worker to be my chauffeur, that would be nice too.

I think part of the reason I write about Host is that I have not gotten to know him well. A good way for us to start would be for Jim and the governor to invite me along on their camping trips.

I have not been camping since I was in grade school, so I would need more equipment than a sleeping bag and flashlight. I'd like a nice RV. After the big trip, I'll be glad to turn it over to the Fish and Wildlife people.

I don't think the state of Kentucky is going to buy me a Mercedes Benz, an RV, or even a sleeping bag, but I do know one thing:

Jim Host will always give me something to write about. Provided I am not someday shot during the "Unbridled Penguin Hunt."

Unbridled Snail Mail

"Mister Postman look and see
If there's a letter in the bag for me."
-The Marvelettes, The Beatles, and The Carpenters

Since Governor Ernie Fletcher has cut off almost every line of communication, your best bet to hear from him is to wait by the mailbox. Fletcher might call people on the telephone; however, I am not on the calling list.

Fletcher has never been much of a glad-hander, as noted by the $5,000 taxpayers paid to install a secret door in his office.

Although much of my writing career has been built upon bashing Governor Fletcher, I had given him credit for his formerly innovative view of technology. I fully supported his Kentucky Connect initiative and the goal to have broadband in every part of Kentucky by 2007.

However, Fletcher has given up the primary tool of the technology era. He announced that he will no longer communicate through email. I can see how Ernie might be a little skittish about email, since emails have been the focus of indictments, embarrassment, and pardons for members of his administration.

Giving up the concept, however, shows a lack of leadership. When leaders are knocked down, they are supposed to jump back up and try again-- not cut and run. It was not the technology, but rather how people chose to use the technology, that caused the governor's problems.

Given enough time and practice, Fletcher and his cronies should be able to produce emails that do not cause grand juries to be convened and pardons to be issued. They will never know until they try.

If the governor gives up modern technology, then all of state government will follow his lead. Soon, the only way to communicate with Frankfort will be through tin cups tied together by string.

When trying to recruit high-tech companies, the slogan "Unbridled Stone Age" will not get the state very far.

Not everyone loves technology like I do. It is hard for me to believe, but there are people in the world who can go several minutes without checking their email.

Voters want to communicate with their leaders quickly and directly. Email is one of the best tools for accomplishing that. When you look at groups like MoveOn.org and similar organizations, you realize what an important tool email has become in our governmental process.

MySpace.com has gotten some negative publicity, but it is a communication source for a whole generation. Fletcher ought to check it out.

I am not asking Fletcher to get on MySpace.com and discuss his sexual preferences. Even I don't do that. Yet, I do have a MySpace.com profile that consists of an old picture of myself, links to two colleagues, and one to William Shatner.

Shatner has sent me emails. If a guy who commanded the Starship Enterprise can drop me a line, then a governor who merely buzzed the United States Capitol can do the same thing.

If Fletcher got a MySpace.com account, I would be glad to let him link to my page. Although I only have five spaces left, Fletcher could be one of my top eight friends. I would even give him my private password, and if the governor is lucky, I might give him Shatner's password as well. I'm sure Bill could give the governor some flying tips.

I will do whatever it takes to get Fletcher interested in email again. I don't think that I am the right person for the job, but I am willing to try.

I know Governor Fletcher likes to use the postal service, seeing as I usually receive a Christmas card from him. I put it up in my office conference room and often leave it up year-round. If the list is long enough to include me, then it must include every other registered voter in Kentucky and maybe even a couple of other states for good measure.

Email would be a lot cheaper, faster, and more effective.

Although a lot of great bands sang the song "Mister Postman," none of them are around today. Snail mail exists, but it is going the way of the telegraph. No one would profit from its comeback, since email is a better alternative.

If Governor Fletcher plans on recruiting high-tech companies to the state, he needs to show that he can talk their language and type an email, even if it means handing out more pardons along the way.

Unbridled Fear Factor

"Fly into the danger zone."
- **Kenny Loggins** (Theme from the movie *Top Gun*)

Having a powerful person mad at you is a danger zone.

I was re-reading Jack Germond's book, *Fat Man in a Middle Seat* (an accurate description of my own air travels), and Germond had an interesting point about President Jimmy Carter.

No one was scared of Jimmy Carter. He came off as wimpy.

People would cower at other presidents but knew Carter would never hurt them.

Governor Ernie Fletcher and Carter have the same problem. No one is afraid of them.

Books about leadership from Machiavelli, to Sun Tzu, to *The Godfather* say the same thing. A leader must have the respect and fear of the people they govern.

No one lives in fear of Ernie Fletcher. He tells people to quit, and they tell him no. Can you imagine someone doing that to Paul Patton, Happy Chandler, or any other governor?

Fletcher was given the ultimate slap in the face. He is the Rodney Dangerfield of Kentucky politics.

Leaders in every walk of life have to establish a "fear factor."

Watch an elementary school teacher who lets children talk in class. Soon, students are throwing paper wads, and eventually they are trying to set the classroom on fire.

Once the teacher loses the fear factor, children will see how far they can push it.   Adults do the same.

If someone thinks they can push a governor around, they will. Most governors never allow that opportunity.

Fletcher gets no respect because he has never done anything to show that he's the ultimate boss. He is bigger on whining than on whippings.

He constantly whines about Attorney General Greg Stumbo, but Stumbo is not worried about what Fletcher is going to do to him.

Fletcher is like the child who runs to the teacher when a bully beats on him. If he struck back and took some bold action, people might take him seriously.

There is a scene in the movie, *Walking Tall,* where a judge releases people that Sheriff Buford Pusser had arrested. Pusser discovered that he was in charge of assigning courthouse office space and moved the judge's chamber to the men's restroom.

Imagine if Fletcher had done that to Lt. Governor Steve Pence.

Instead, Pence sits in his nice office, collecting his nice salary, embarrassing the guy who got him his job. Pence knows Fletcher is not mean enough to hurt him.

I would have loved to have seen Pence try his partial resignation with Paul Patton. Patton would have assigned Pence office space in another country. Like Afghanistan.

When Patton was governor, he lambasted University of Kentucky President Charlie Wethington in front of a large crowd. Wethington sat and took it. He was not about to make Paul Patton madder than he already was.

A former fighter pilot should understand the psychology of tough leadership. I don't think Fletcher ever flew in combat, but if he did, how would he have handled it? Would he have been heroic like Tom Cruise's character in *Top Gun*, or would he have whined and said the other country's pilots were conducting a political witch-hunt?

An incumbent governor has so much power that, even under indictment, it should be impossible to lose the office.

That calculation is based on the fear factor. If contractors can give money to opposing candidates and not be in fear of losing business, the power of incumbency is lost. If state employees can campaign against an incumbent governor with no trepidation about losing their jobs, the incumbent loses the fear factor.

Fletcher's crew tried to play it cute when they were putting their political appointees in jobs. It got him into the merit hiring scandal that plagued his administration.

He would have been better off being open about his desire to flex his political muscle.

It is better for leaders to be feared than loved. Fletcher is in the unique position of not being either.

Unless Fletcher can get people to respect and fear him, his danger zone is going to be his re-election campaign.

Kentucky's Calling Harry Truman

"America's Calling Harry Truman: Harry, could you please come home?"
- **Chicago**

After Inspector General Bobby Russell did a wonderful job of finding waste, fraud and abuse in the Kentucky Transportation Department, Governor Fletcher's cronies responded by firing him.

I guess they did not want Bobby reading the stuff they had in their emails.

Kentucky ought to look at forming a bi-partisan commission to study waste and fraud within the state, like the committee Senator Harry Truman headed to find waste in the military during World War II."

Unlike Governor Fletcher, Truman actually found waste, fraud and abuse. In fact, he found billions of dollars of it and put several people in jail.

Harry Truman is my political hero. My high school required a senior thesis, and I did mine on the election of 1948. Truman is my idea of what a politician should be.

Kentucky could use him now.

Imagine if the ghost of Harry Truman could come back in Ernie Fletcher's body. Kentucky's scandals would go away.

Truman had a sign on his desk that read, "The buck stops here." He said, "If you can't take the heat, stay out of the kitchen."

Truman was progressive in promoting civil rights legislation. In fact, part of the Democratic party led by Senator Strom Thurmond broke off and started a third political party in protest of Truman's stand for equality.

I can't imagine Truman standing by, like Governor Fletcher has, and allowing the Transportation Department to employ only five African Americans out of the 317 people that it has hired.

When Truman ended segregation in the armed forces, he said, "If we were sending colored soldiers (the language of race was different then) to die in war, we would not force them to be segregated."

Governor Fletcher, as the leader of the National Guard, has been color blind as to which Kentuckians put their lives on the line in Iraq. People of all races can fight in Iraq, but if you are African American, do not expect to come back to a job at the Transportation Department.

Unless you can prove that you are a well-connected, registered Republican.

Truman did not care about partisanship; he wanted the best person to get the job done. He brought in former Republican President Herbert Hoover to head up an important commission, and Hoover did a terrific job.

Fletcher blames all his mistakes on Democrats and screams "politics" if someone questions his actions. He would be better served mirroring Harry Truman and using wisdom, not politics as a measure of who he listens to.

There is a lot of knowledge amongst the governors who preceded Fletcher, but none of them are standing by waiting for his call. Fletcher surrounds himself with young brats with Game Boys and Blackberrys instead of senior advisors who know the ropes.

Truman asked knowledgeable people like General George Marshall and Dean Atchison to assist him. He did not care about their politics.

Harry Truman made the toughest choice a president ever had to make—deciding to use the atomic bomb, twice.

I don't remember Truman hiding from the media in another country after he dropped the bomb. He stayed in Washington and dealt with the criticism.

He did daily outdoor walks and did not have a secret door to his office.

Truman's life experiences before he became president made him who he was as a leader. He got a late start in politics after serving in World War I and failing as a haberdasher. He never went to college and had a connection with common people that came from hard knocks.

Truman's background made him the perfect guy to head up a commission to find waste in government. If Truman were running Kentucky and had had an inspector general show him the state being soaked for millions of dollars, the general would not have been fired, he would have received a medal.

Truman would not have made allowances for political contributors who did wrong. He would have given them hell.

Or as Truman would say, "I give them the truth and they think its hell."

Lighting a Fire like Reagan

"Come on baby, light my fire. Try to set the night on fire"
- The Doors

The Doors could always attract attention. The band had a short career with only a few major hits (the group was dying before Jim Morrison did), yet they managed to make a permanent mark on history.

Just like the song, the Doors were able to light a fire by focusing on big ideas and making their own mark.

Big ideas are important in every field, especially in government.

The American Experience on PBS did a wonderful series about Ronald Reagan. Reagan is one of the few Republicans, and only Republican presidential candidate, I have ever voted for.

Many fellow Democrats never understood what I saw in Reagan. I disagreed with many of Reagan's social policies and was closer to Reagan's opponent, Walter Mondale, on several issues.

What I liked about Reagan is that he knew where he wanted to lead us.

He had a vision of where he wanted America to go and did a wonderful job of communicating that vision.

Reagan was not given credit as being an intellectual, but he had a tremendous grasp of history. Being our oldest president may have helped. By the time Reagan took office at age 71, he had had a ton of unique life experiences. He wanted to make a mark, which he did.

Love him or hate him, Ronald Reagan is one of the defining presidents in America's history. Reagan's view of the world was not a "vision thing" that some political consultant dreamed up.

The contrast with Reagan is what frustrates me about Kentucky Governor Ernie Fletcher. I have asked many people, including those close to Fletcher, to articulate the governor's vision for Kentucky. No one can tell me.

They throw out slogans like "Unbridled Spirit" or "Stop waste, fraud and abuse." Although they can hand out a laundry list of issues and stances, they can never give me a comprehensive vision.

I have been hard on Governor Fletcher and will continue to be. I want him to be Ronald Reagan.

I do not expect Fletcher to have Reagan's ability to command a crowd. Few politicians have Reagan's oratory gifts. Ironically, the one who comes closest is Bill Clinton. It is unfair to compare a doctor-fighter pilot to a trained movie actor.

I want Fletcher to have a vision. I want him to tell me why Kentuckians will look back years from now and note his administration. I want him to tell me how he wants his obituary to read.

I just want some leadership.

I once compared a former romantic interest of mine to a Doors concert. It could be the best experience of your life or the worst experience of your life, but it was never going to be mediocre.

I don't want Fletcher to be mediocre. I want a great plan, even if I don't agree with it.

To people of a certain age, The Doors will always be a part of life. A *Rolling Stone Magazine* cover of Jim Morrison in the 1980's summed it up perfectly—"He's Hot, He's Beautiful, He's Dead."

Years after Morrison's demise, his influence on popular culture remains timeless.

I want Governor Fletcher to do something that will have a timeless influence.

I want him to do something that will light Kentuckians' fire.

Succession Ain't Working Anymore

"The whiskey ain't working anymore."
- Travis Tritt and Marty Stuart

I do not think Governor Ernie Fletcher is a whiskey drinker, but if there were ever a governor who needed a drink, Fletcher would be the one.

With things already going badly for the governor, the humiliation and embarrassment resulting from events such as his refuted attempt to fire Lieutenant Governor Pence have not helped his credibility as Kentucky's commander and chief.

If I were governor, I would smash a whiskey bottle over Pence's head and then pardon myself for it. Instead, Fletcher looks like a guy who needs a double--maybe make that a triple shot of whiskey.

The United States repealed the Prohibition Amendment in 1933, giving the governor the choice to have a drink if he desires one.

Kentuckians should repeal another amendment: the one that permits governors to succeed themselves and forces the lieutenant governor and governor to run as a slate. Thus far, the amendment has been a disaster.

Before the amendment was enacted, the system was simple. All constitutional officers, including the governor, were elected for one four-year term. The lieutenant governor was elected separately to preside over the state Senate and to spend the next four years campaigning for his or her own term as governor.

Many lieutenant governors went on to be elected as governor. Prior to their election, Patton, Jones, Collins, Carroll, and Ford had first served as lieutenant governor. Even if you were never elected governor, being lieutenant governor was a pretty good gig. The lieutenant governor had a mansion, a staff, police escorts, and a personal chef.

Yet after succession passed, the lieutenant governor was required to run on a slate with a gubernatorial candidate, and the duty of presiding over the state Senate was taken away. Shortly thereafter, the mansion disappeared, and the personal chef was nowhere to be found.

Since most governors plan to run for re-election, the lieutenant governor now has eight years to do nothing. Attracting quality talent to a "do-nothing job" without the perks of a mansion or chef is not easily done.

If you compare the resumes of candidates who ran for lieutenant governor prior to succession with those who came after, you'll find that the resumes of those before are far superior.

Prior to the succession amendment, almost every lieutenant governor in recent decades had been elected to a public office (and several even held statewide offices) before serving as lieutenant governor. Neither Pence nor Charlie Owen, the slated candidate for the Democratic Party, had ever been elected to any position prior to running for lt. governor.

Although a big resume is not required to maintain a deathwatch on the governor, one would at least expect that two people elected on the same slate would have a close working relationship. This has yet to be seen.

Each of the post-succession lt. governors —Steve Henry and Steve Pence—have had public falling-outs with the governors who selected them. When lieutenant governors ran separately from the governor, no one cared. Now the recent actions of lieutenant governor Pence reflect poorly on both himself and on Fletcher as well.

All of this leads to the conclusion that it is time to forget about constitutional officers succeeding themselves and forcing governors and lieutenant governors to run on slates.

There were supposed to be big advantages to succession. Someone please remind me of what they were.

It would be better if Kentucky went back to the old system. Then, governors would have to make hard decisions rather than beginning the re-election campaign the first day they enter office. No one would care if the lieutenant governor stabbed the governor in the back because they are not on the same team anyway.

Several years ago, people made a strong argument for placing term limits on congressmen. The same logic now holds true for governors.

An entrenched incumbent who can give out goodies, jobs, and contracts is hard to blast out of office. A single four-year term would force governors to quit focusing on re-election and compel them to implement the promised changes that got them into office, like eliminating waste, fraud, and abuse.

Governor Fletcher knows that drinking is not the answer to his problems.

Whiskey does not work and neither does the succession amendment.

Long-Haired Freaky People
Need Not Apply

"And the sign said,
Long-haired freaky people
Need not apply."
- The song "Signs" by the Five Man Electrical Band

The 1971 song "Signs" strikes a chord with many people because it points out society's intolerance for diversity. Yet I do not expect the Kentucky Parks Department to be pumping "Signs" through the Muzak at the state parks this year.

Recently, the parks commissioner issued an edict stating that in order for park employees to keep their jobs, they had to be neat and clean, meaning no tattoos, no long hair on men, no body piercing, and shirt tails tucked in.

Although tattoos, long hair, and body piercing are ways for people to express themselves, the park commissioner's message discourages such forms of individuality. The message instead encourages the mentality that looks overshadow performance when it comes to job evaluation.

When I finished graduate school in 1982, the only job that I could find was on the clean-up crew at the Kentucky Horse Park. There was an unspoken selection process that took place. All of the "long-haired freaky people" were given the jobs on the clean-up crew while the attractive-looking people worked at the front desk. Unless they have increased the pay, I cannot imagine where the commissioner is going to find enough well-groomed people willing to clean up horse stalls and pick up trash for a profession.

I suspect the grooming policy is illegal and outright wrong. It is prejudice at its very worst. I cannot fathom a court agreeing with the dismissal of a merit employee for having long hair or tattoos. I expect that the policy will cost the state a lot in legal expenses.

In many parts of Kentucky, the state park is one of the largest employers, and a park job is hard to come by. It provides steady employment with good benefits, and in exchange, career employees have to deal with bosses and policies changing at least every four years.

One of the most humiliating parts of my clean-up crew experience was working for a boss who was verbally abusive and lazy. He got his job through his political connections rather than for his ability or experience. A lot of park employees are forced to cope with unprofessional bosses and other traumatic job-related issues. Now they have to look sharp as well.

I also noticed that the same news release pointed out that the Parks Department is making a big push to fight "waste, fraud, and abuse." I am a little unclear about the correlation. Are people with tattoos less honest than those who do not have them? Do men with earrings and women with nose rings feel the need to steal to feed their piercing habit? How much do tattoos and piercings cost? Maybe well-groomed people really don't steal, but if so, how do they explain all the well-groomed people involved in scandals on Wall Street?

One of my first employees was a Summa Cum Laude graduate of the University of Kentucky. Coming from a modest background, he worked his way through Hazard Community College and UK by crawling under coal trucks and changing the oil. He had an incredible work ethic. He was one of the finest people I have ever known, even with an earring, beard, and hair down to his waist. Apparently, he wouldn't cut it with the Kentucky Parks Department, but any other employer would be lucky to have him.

If my current career ends, I am still eligible to get my old job back cleaning up the Horse Park. I do not have enough hair to grow it long, and I am scared of any kind of body piercing.

However, the provision also stated that shirttails need to be tucked in. I could be in trouble there.

I suspect that if you go into the kitchen of every five-star hotel or restaurant in the country, you are going to find people with long hair, tattoos, or body piercing. Creative people, like chefs, like to display their individuality, and successful businesses want the best people no matter what they look like.

The people running the parks need to go back to evaluating employees by the job they do, not by how they wear their hair and jewelry. Or as Charlie Daniels said, "If you don't like the way I'm looking, you just leave this long-haired country boy alone."

Parks Commissioner in Wrong Country

"I love her; she loves me; but I don't fit in her society.
Lord have mercy on the boy from down in the boondocks."
- Joe South

Throughout history, snobs have looked down on working people.

British shows and movies like *Upstairs, Downstairs* and *Gosford Park* illustrate the pressures placed upon the serving class to not interact with those they serve.

We are different in America. We don't have kings and queens. Family history can help someone become president, but the White House has been open to peanut farmers, movie actors, and people with working-class roots. We like people who come from "down in the boondocks."

The guy running the Kentucky Parks Department must have wound up in the wrong country. He sent out an edict stating that they would fire park employees who had long hair, earrings, or their shirttails untucked.

It turns out the guy was serious, and he fired three people who cleaned a state park. Two were single mothers, and one was a Navy veteran with tattoos.

The park workers' supervisor has resigned over the policy. He deserves our admiration, but that still is not going to feed his family.

As far as the veteran is concerned, he was good enough to fight for our country but not allowed to keep a job that paid $6.30 an hour.

After his first edict, the commissioner then denied employees the opportunity to stay the same parks where they work.

 The Commissioner's Office said, "Is a guest going to be comfortable mingling with someone who turns out to be a guest and an employee?"

I'm missing something here. Maybe in England people get outraged if they find out that they are sharing a hotel with someone who works there. Here in America, I don't think anyone really cares. In fact, how would someone know? I go to state parks but usually interact with whomever I came with. I have no idea who the other guests are unless they turn their television up at 3 a.m.

Maybe the state parks have been having swinging singles mixers like Club Med, and the commissioner wants to make sure he has the right combination of people. Since the commissioner came in to try to make the parks profitable, he might have a secret plan to have cocktail hours and singles nights. They don't sell cocktails at state parks, but maybe he could get people to mill around the ice cream machine instead.

Rather than just being a snobby elitist, the commissioner may have a shrewd business strategy.

Holiday Inn and other hotels give discounts when their employees' families stay in their hotels. Most airlines let their employees fly free, and it has never bothered me to sit next to a pilot or flight attendant.

The governor got a number of votes from people with long hair, tattoos, earrings and body piercing. I will bet that Fletcher also got some votes from parks employees and their families. He can kiss those votes goodbye now.

If Kentucky were like England, where you stay king for life, the governor would not have to worry. Here in America, everyone has a say in deciding who runs things.

Even if they have long hair, earrings, body piercing, and dress like slobs.

Rednecks, White Socks, and Blue Ribbon Beer

"There's no place that I would rather be than right here,
with rednecks, white socks, and Blue Ribbon Beer"
- Johnny Russell

Growing up, the political parties were simple. Elections took place every six months. Republicans were people who belonged to country clubs. Democrats were people who worked for people who belonged to country clubs.

My parents owned two bars, and their patrons voted every year for Democrats. Rednecks, white socks, and Blue Ribbon beer described the clientele. As time went on, those people started voting for Republicans.

Next year there will be no elections in Kentucky. It will be a bad year for political consultants but a good time to figure out why many candidates use them in the first place.

Most "Washington consultants" (consultants who claim to be from Washington, even if they just visited D.C. on a bus tour) are of the same ilk. They drop names of the "important" people they've met, act like know-it-alls, push volunteers out of the way, and direct all the campaign money into things that make them a commission.

They don't care if the candidate wins or loses. As soon as the campaign is over, they skip town and find the next sucker.

Consultants like to use gimmicks that worked in previous campaigns for their newest clients. Rather than look at local issues, they bring in the gimmick of the week.

Kentucky Democrats had an issue that could bring working-class people back to the party, but I never heard a candidate mention it this fall.

Earlier this summer, the Kentucky Parks Commissioner started firing state parks employees who had long hair, tattoos, or their shirttails hanging out. He also said that parks employees could not visit the parks where they work in their free time.

I went on a talk show to discuss the issue. I said that the ordeal would really hurt Republicans in the next election. Caller after caller phoned in and said I was wrong. I was.

The state Democratic Party made a push to promote the issue, but few candidates picked up on it. I guess their consultants convinced the candidates to ignore it.

The park firings were a classic cultural symbol. It was the rich boss telling poor people what they needed to look like and where they could hang out.

The question "Will you fire someone for having long hair or a tattoo?" would have been tough for Republican candidates to answer. It never got asked.

Instead, the Republicans pushed their own cultural issues as a way to fire up supporters. They controlled the political agenda. The Democratic candidates and their high-priced consultants let them do it.

Many Democrats went on television and said they were for the same issues that the Republicans were for. The result was the same across the board: those candidates lost.

Why vote for someone whose response is "me too?" The Republicans had better consultants who developed issues and let the Democrats react.

The Democratic Party has been the party of working people. If candidates had been pushing the value of hard work over grooming, it would have made a difference.

I can't imagine someone with a tattoo or long hair voting for someone who wants to fire them.

If the people who used to hang out in my parents' bars had heard about the park firings, they would have voted for the Democrats.

Those people would value how a person works, not how they look. The ability to express themselves with long hair or a tattoo is a freedom they would fight for. Tolerance means not firing someone because they have their shirttail out. Family values means not firing good workers, especially ones with children to support.

If some of the Democrats had brought up the park firings, they would have been discussing their own culture and values, rather than reacting to issues proposed by the other side.

In my first column about the parks firings, I used a song lyric: "The sign said, long-haired freaky people, need not apply."

Although high-priced consultants don't get it, working people understand the message of that song.

Especially rednecks in white socks who drink Blue Ribbon beer.

Unbridled Super Cop

"She doesn't like the tough guys,
She says that they all got brains where they sit"
- REO Speedwagon

For several weeks, the Kentucky State Police ran a television advertisement encouraging people not to drink and drive. The ad ended with a shot of Lt. Governor Steve Pence surrounded by policemen.

Pence should not have been in the ad.   Taxpayers should not pay for politicians to promote themselves. I do not think that any elected official should have been in the commercial; however, if you absolutely had to pick one, Pence would be a good choice.

In addition to being the lt. governor, Pence is the head of the Kentucky Justice Cabinet. He is a former federal prosecutor and currently serves as a military judge. Pence's professional life has been devoted to law enforcement.

The ad ran again but without Pence this time. Instead, Governor Ernie Fletcher took his place. "Mr. Law and Order" was replaced by a man who recently told a grand jury that he refused to answer questions on the grounds that he may incriminate himself.

This is equivalent to a television show like *Law and Order* recasting one of its main characters with O.J. Simpson.

If the commercial's goal is to scare people out of driving drunk, then you need real law enforcement personalities encouraging people, not politicians.

Even though Pence is an elected official, he looks like someone you do not want to mess with. The commercial makes him look like Buford Pusser in a business suit, whereas Fletcher looks like Barney Fife. An intoxicated person might be scared of Pence, but no one is going to be scared of Fletcher.

Inebriated Kentuckians will see Fletcher and figure that driving drunk is not any worse than noodling. Fletcher lumps all misdemeanors into the same category as catching fish with your hands.

Republican drinkers will believe that if they get into trouble, Ernie will let them off with a pardon or at the very least help them get a state job.

The advertisement dumped Pence around the same time Fletcher handed out pardons to his indicted cronies. It was well known that Pence did not agree with the governor's actions. I wonder if Fletcher yanked Pence from the ad as a form of punishment for disagreeing with his decision to grant the pardons.

It is obvious that Fletcher was added to the commercial with hasty editing. The latest commercial reminds me of a bad Kung Fu movie that has been poorly overdubbed into English.

Mothers Against Drunk Driving (MADD) has been one of the most effective organizations founded in my lifetime. They have made a major impact on the way society treats drunk drivers.

Politicians like Fletcher want to be associated with a popular cause.

I do not know how much the state spent on the commercial with Fletcher, but it has been on almost every time that I have turned on the television.

The state spent over $645,000 for its "Unbridled Spirit" logo. I hope Kentuckians paid less for Fletcher to play "Unbridled Super Cop."

Trey Grayson's Unbridled Ambition

"But you're too young to know the score, so come back when you're older."
- Donny Osmond

When my father was dying of cancer, he said he wasn't worried about not going to Heaven. "If God grades on a curve, I am in," he said. "I have seen the competition."

Governor Ernie Fletcher, a minister, never sought theological advice from my father, a professional gambler. But if Heaven to Fletcher is the Kentucky governorship, he might espouse a viewpoint similar to my dad's.

If voters grade on a curve, he could have a second term. At the very least, he will be the Republican nominee.

I'm writing this nine months until the primary. If there were another Republican planning on beating Fletcher, they would either need to be a multi-millionaire or have already begun their campaign two years ago.

Trey Grayson does not fall into either category.

The Republican establishment is unhappy with Governor Fletcher. Lt. Governor Steve Pence, Senate President David Williams, and

United States Senator Mitch McConnell have dropped some not-so-subtle hints that Fletcher should find something else to do with his life.

They have a problem. Fletcher is not listening to them. He keeps running for re-election.

Secretary of State Trey Grayson announced that he is considering a bid to run against Fletcher.

I don't know Grayson well, but I've followed his career. Like me, he grew up in suburban Kenton County, and he went to the same high school that my sister attended. My parents knew his parents, and I met Trey when he worked for my friend Bob Babbage.

Babbage told me years ago that Grayson would get elected to something someday. Bob was right. He has a great chance to be governor but not in 2007.

There are two scenarios for Grayson. One is that Fletcher stays in the race for governor. The second is that Fletcher drops out.

If Fletcher stays in, the 34-year-old Grayson will face an incumbent in a party primary. If Fletcher drops out, more seasoned Republicans like Pence, Williams, or one (or more) of the congressional delegation will jump in the race.

In either case, Grayson will have problems.

It is easy for a secretary of state, surrounded by fawning staff and well-wishers, to think that it is just a simple jump to become governor. The secretary of state walks by the governor's office every day. Or at least sees the secret door that hides it.

There is a lot of young political talent in Northern Kentucky, and some like Grayson or Covington Vice Mayor Rob Sanders (who was recently elected Kenton County Commonwealth Attorney) will make a splash at the statewide level. Their success, however, will hinge upon picking the right race at the right time.

I've often made the case that if Todd Hollenbach had run for lieutenant governor in 1975 instead of governor, he would have eventually won the governorship. It was the same situation with George Atkins in 1979, Grady Stumbo in 1983, and Floyd Poore in 1991.

Once they lost the gubernatorial bid, they were never elected to anything else.

I would hate to see that happen to Grayson.

Machiavelli said that if you're going to make an attempt on a king's life, you have to kill him. Unless Trey has huge financial resources or support from organizations that I don't know about, he is better off waiting.

Taking out a sitting governor in nine months is almost impossible. I don't care if the governor is indicted, and every major officeholder in the Republican Party is blasting him.

A sitting governor has a lot of power. The governor dominates news coverage and has a large staff and contractors beholden to him.

I would hate to see Grayson throw away a promising career. I hope he waits and comes back when he is older and more seasoned.

One of the two governors from Northern Kentucky was William Goebel, who was shot while he took the oath of office.

I hope that Grayson's unbridled ambition does not shoot a hole in his chance to become the third.

Larry Forgy, the GOP Answer To Gatewood Galbraith

"The game of life is hard to play,
I'm going to lose it anyway."
- **Suicide** (theme to the movie and television show *M*A*S*H*)

After three or four seasons on *M*A*S*H*, McLean Stevenson left the television show to become a star on his own.

He had a sitcom called *Hello Larry* that lasted about six weeks. *M*A*S*H* went on to become one of the most popular shows of all times.

Stevenson became the Hollywood symbol of a loser. If McLean was in a show, you knew it was going to bomb.

Larry Forgy is the McLean Stevenson of Kentucky politics.

If Forgy runs for office, you know he is going to lose.

Rumors once circulated that Governor Fletcher was going to replace Commerce Secretary Jim Host with Forgy.

I wish he would have. It would have given me tons to write about.

When Host resigned, I was very sad. Host had been the subject of some of my most popular columns.

Whether he was firing state park workers with long hair or spending millions on the "Unbridled Spirit" logo, Host always did something to make me mad.

Host had the same problem in state government that I would have if I were a public official. I've run my own business, and I am used to doing things my own way. Host is a self-made millionaire used to running his business and ignoring social niceties.

If I were in state government, some columnist would be bashing on me.

I don't know Host, but our mutual friend Al Smith tells me I would like him.

I would certainly do a business deal with him. He knows how to make money. I was getting to where I liked him, and it was killing my column.

Bringing Forgy in would have been a godsend. He can't resist a microphone and will always say something stupid.

He is the perfect grist for a struggling columnist.

It would have a brilliant political move for Fletcher. People would be so busy bashing Forgy that they would forget Fletcher exists.

Forgy plays an important role in the Republican Party. He is their clown prince and perennial candidate, like Gatewood Galbraith is for the Democrats.

I will argue that Gatewood has had a better political career.

Compare Forgy to Gatewood.

In 1983, Gatewood ran for commissioner of agriculture and lost. Forgy thought about running for governor but didn't.

Gatewood ran, Forgy didn't. Score one for Gatewood.

In 1987, Forgy started to run for governor and suddenly quit. He got over what caused him to quit by 1991 and lost the primary. He lost again in 1995.

Gatewood also ran for governor three times. He didn't win but never dropped out. He ran for Congress and lost too.

You have to give Gatewood the edge on persistence.

In 2000, Forgy ran for the Supreme Court. With George W. Bush leading the ticket, a Republican like Forgy should have walked into it. Instead, he was completely humiliated.

To top it off, his sister also ran for Congress. She lost too.

I've voted for Gatewood several times. Like the majority of Kentuckians, I have never voted for Forgy.

Gatewood admits to smoking a lot of dope. A toke or two might take the edge off of Forgy.

Forgy finally quit running for office, but Gatewood kept plugging away. Gatewood never wins, but he doesn't go around whining about it either.

Forgy lashes out at everybody and everything. He is really sad. He's worked for so many law firms that they ought to issue him office space by the hour.

He could have used the gig as commerce secretary. It would have given him a steady income and media attention.

It would have also given me something new to write about. Forgy has pulled stunt after stunt to get himself in the news.

Since McLean Stevenson is dead, targeting Forgy is really my best bet. Forgy would run down the street naked if he thought it would get him media coverage, and he constantly does things to provide fodder for my columns.

Hello Larry will finally be a hit.

(I included this to show that some other doctors who have entered politics don't understand the concept of public perception.)

The Not-So-Blind Trust

"It's always been a matter of trust"
- Billy Joel

One of the most important positions in the world is the majority leader in the United States Senate.

It's only a few steps from majority leader to president. Lyndon Johnson made it. Bob Dole and others tried.

Current Majority Leader Bill Frist has his eye on the White House. He may be looking at a stay in the big house instead.

Frist comes from an incredibly rich family. His father and brother founded Hospital Corporation of America (HCA), the nation's largest hospital chain. Senator Frist disclosed that he is worth somewhere between $7 million and $35 million.

You won't find him in the line to get a payday loan.

Like many rich people, he owns stock that can be worth more or less depending on the decisions that the government makes.

Most wealthy senators, including Frist, put their money in something called a "blind trust." They turn their money over to someone else, and they are not supposed to know how it is invested.

I know a lot about blind trusts. One of my friends ran for governor of Kentucky several years ago and asked me to manage his blind trust if he won.

If I ran through the money, he wouldn't know until he got out of office.

I was honored but stressed. I would have been responsible for him and his family. If I were to have screwed up, his kids would not have gone to college.

He lost the election, but his children will be well-educated.

Jimmy Carter did a really stupid thing with his blind trust. He put Billy Carter, his beer-swilling redneck brother, in charge.

Jimmy lost re-election and found that Billy's shrewd money management had cause him to go broke and fall heavily into debt. Jimmy had to start writing books to get out of hock.

Frist does not have Carter's problem. His family knows how to handle money. The question is whether or not they know tricks that hurt the public.

Two possible scandals have erupted for Senator Frist. The first centers around the senator and HCA being investigated by the Securities and Exchange Commission and the Justice Department for possible insider trading.

Senator Frist was able to sell his HCA stock right before it dropped by 15%. The senator was either tipped off or incredibly lucky.

Insider trading is the same thing that Martha Stewart went to jail for. She went for chump change. If found guilty, Frist would be looking at a serious sentence.

Company executives have to sit tight when they have information that the public doesn't know about. People will not buy stocks if they think the market is rigged.

Friends of Frist say that he would not have done something illegal because he is rich. He does not need the money.

ANYONE accused of insider trading is rich. It is a crime committed by wealthy stockholders and their friends at the country club.

You don't see people on food stamps being accused of insider trading.

When the Justice Department stops by HCA to drop off a subpoena, you know that things are very serious.

Especially since the leaders at the Justice Department were appointed by Frist's close friend George W. Bush.

Insider traders have to be stupid since technology makes it easy to catch them. If HCA did wrong, we will know.

A bigger concern is that Frist's blind trust had a seeing-eye dog-- Senator Frist himself.

Numerous documents show that Frist kept a close eye on his money. He was actively involved in many of the "blind" trust decisions, including the one to dump the HCA.

The blind trust seemed to have 20/20 vision.

Along with being greedy, Frist might be a liar.

In a 2003 television interview, he said that "As far as I know, I own no HCA stock." Two weeks before that interview, the trustee had given Frist an update on the HCA stock he owned.

Frist is in a position where he affects every American. Forget the fact that he is dying to be president; he has a huge amount of power right now.

He can use his power to help us or use it to line his pocket. If he is going to stay a United States senator, he needs to show that he is obeying the law.

It is a matter of trust.

Part II

Unbridled Issues We
Ought to Be Talking About

History Teachers Who Don't Know History

"Don't Know Much About History"
- Sam Cooke

About 20 years ago, I was asked to speak to a college business class. During my lecture,I told the class they should stop studying business and start studying history and English instead.

I was never invited back.

In business, one must understand where their market has been and where it is going. Through the exploration of history, a person can analyze these trends.

I have a passion for history--a fire that was lit by tremendous high school history teachers and college professors.

Chester Finn Jr., my former professor at Vanderbilt and an education guru, noted that only 31% of middle school history teachers and 41% of high school history teachers actually majored in history.

It may be necessary for middle school teachers to gain a knowledge of several fields, but I am horrified at the poor percentage of high school history teachers with degrees in history.

Yet, I do not blame the teachers but rather the administration who hire them.

While in college, I continually met students who despised history. For me, hating history was like hating pizza or the American flag. It was hard to imagine someone who could not love history.

When I asked why, I learned that many had had high school teachers with no background or interest in history. The "teachers" made their students memorize dates and random facts instead of teaching them history.

Students subjected to classes like these should be able to sue the school for malpractice and have the school administrators arrested for torture.

History is about great people, events, and movements in life.

My two high school teachers, Tim Banker and Joe Hackett, could not have been more different from each another. In comparison, Hackett and Banker were like salt and vinegar. On the surface they did not sound like a good combination; however, their taste for knowledge had me striving to become a better student and made me a fan of history.

Banker, a funny, left-handed Irishman, coached football and track. During my junior year, I became Banker's favorite student because I too was Irish, left-handed, funny, played football, and ran track. Surprisingly, however, I was an unlikely candidate for becoming the teacher's pet.

Entering my junior year of high school, I ranked 110th out of a class of 128. I played sports, but did not have natural athletic ability. My friends were comprised of the top five students in the class and the worst five students in the class. The police were on a first-name basis with the bottom five and were quickly learning my name too.

Banker helped me become excited about history and school in general, and in the process, I became a good student and drifted away from the negative crowd.

On top of knowing his history, Banker was a great entertainer. Banker believed learning should be fun, and his teaching methods never lead to a dull class.

However, there was nothing fun about my other mentor, Joe Hackett. I have never known a tougher disciplinarian than him.

Hackett had been a meat cutter in Covington and did not graduate from college until he was nearly 50.

Hackett coached state champion baseball teams, and I suspect his talent as a baseball coach kept him from getting fired. Hackett, a registered socialist and teacher in a conservative Catholic school, challenged and intimidated all of his students despite their social class and parents' connections.

Hackett stressed that the powerful must be challenged or they will trample over the rights of the less powerful. I never left his class being afraid to challenge authority. I was only afraid of him.

I was privileged to be the first person to receive an award named in his honor. Hackett and I stayed in touch for the rest of his life, but he was not my buddy: he was my teacher and mentor.

Every adolescent and young adult should have teachers like Banker and Hackett—teachers with passion who actually study and believe in what they are teaching instead of just scrambling to stay one chapter ahead of their students.

The song "Don't Know Much about History" should be seen as entertainment rather than the theme song for America's teachers.

If I were in charge of education, administrators who hire history teachers that don't know history would only have to remember one date—their termination date. It would be listed under "current events."

Kentucky Gets an F in World History

"It's the end of the world as we know it."
- REM

The Thomas B. Fordham Institute recently released a report entitled, "The State of State World History Standards for 2006." The report gave all 50 states a letter grade based on their world history education standards.

I have often complained about the lack of focus on American history in Kentucky schools.   It looks like the study of world history is even worse. Kentucky received an F.

Chester Finn Jr., President of the Thomas B. Fordham Institute, was one of my favorite professors at Vanderbilt University. I know from personal experience that he does not give out a lot of A's (at least not to me), but he also does not give out F's lightly either.

If Kentucky received an F from Professor Finn, we are in big trouble. As much as I would like Kentucky to impress my former teacher, what really concerns me is whether or not Kentucky can compete in a world economy.

In a world where the global and local economies are interconnected, it is vital to know something about the culture, people, and places with which we do business. However, I am afraid that we do not know much about our neighbors.

Terms like immigration, globalization, and world economy are the hot buzz words in the business world. In order to understand these terms, a person needs to be aware of the world's history and its diverse cultures.

Finn and Martin Davis' foreword to the report noted, "Nations that were little more than curiosities to most Americans have transformed themselves into places of vital interest and concern to us."

Yet, disappointingly, Kentucky high schools and colleges are not giving history the attention it deserves. Many American business people and educators need to realize that ignoring history could potentially put American companies out of business and push the nation into an economic recession.

Almost every Fortune 1000 company has a division of its operations located outside of the United States. The advancement of technology and communications will continue to cause this number to rise steadily.

A person cannot turn on talk radio without hearing an argument concerning immigration. I wonder if the people beating their chests know anything about the history of the people trying to enter the United States or the history of the immigrants who came to this country over the past 200 years.

It would help if they understood the long history of people fleeing economic depravity and social injustice to come to the United States. As long as we pride ourselves on being the symbol of freedom and opportunity, people with ambition will want to join us.

Over the years, I have done business with people in India and Great Britain. Having a working knowledge of their history and culture has allowed me to break down many communications barriers.

The international community understands American history. However, we know little about the world's history.

If an American can tell me who the Prime Minster of India is without looking it up, email me, and let me know. I may not send a prize, but I will give them a personal A in current events.

If you are familiar with a person or a community's history and customs, then you can identify and understand their ideas, hopes, desires and motivations--information that is pivotal for businesses to know in order to sell their products.

I hope the big fat F on the Fordham Institute Report card serves as a wake up call for Kentucky. It is a problem that can be fixed.

The report awarded our neighboring state of Virginia with an A.

Unless we get our act together, multi-national corporations are going to turn to places like Virginia for employees instead of Kentucky.

We need to start teaching world history and teaching it correctly. If not, it will be the end of the world as we know it.

The $2000 Aspirin

"No pill's going to cure my ills."
- Robert Palmer

When I started in the financial planning business 24 years ago, many of my clients were doctors.

I had a group of emergency room doctors tell me the same story over and over.

A person on Medicaid would have a headache and want aspirin. Rather than buy one, they would call an ambulance, have the ambulance take them to the emergency room, and get the hospital to give them aspirin.

If they had gone to a store, they would have had to pay for the aspirin. Since they went to the hospital, aspirin was free.

That stunt cost the state about $2000 a visit.

It was a horrible abuse, but no one had a way to stop it. Someone always takes advantage of a system designed to help people.

I'm sure the people who called the ambulances patted themselves on the back. They saved the dollar it would take to buy aspirin.

They did not care that it cost their neighbors $2000.

These days, my clients are horribly injured people.

If they get cut off Medicaid, they die. They have no other way of paying for the health care they need.

Medicaid is becoming a bigger and bigger chunk of every state budget. Health care costs are going up, and the population is aging and in need of more and more treatment.

I am like most people when it comes to health care. I want the best-educated doctors, the newest and most innovative medicines, and hospitals that provide service like Four Seasons Hotels.

I just don't want to pay for it.

As an employer, I am keenly aware of how fast health care costs are going up. As a taxpayer, I know that Medicaid is taking up a chunk of money that I would like to spend on better schools or better roads.

My health insurance premiums went up about 20% last year. You know what I will do? Pay it.

I live in fear of getting sick and wiping out my life savings. Most people feel the same way.

Many people on Medicaid have a different fear--being cut off of Medicaid and dying.

That is why those on Medicaid should be the most angry when people waste money on a $2000 aspirin.

The jerks are jeopardizing their lives.

When politicians propose solutions for the huge cost of Medicaid, they often have ideas that penalize everyone in the system.

It is a like a teacher keeping an entire class after school because one person threw a paper wad.

One popular proposal would force everyone on Medicaid to re-apply for coverage. That is a terrible idea. It penalizes those who aren't good at filling out paperwork.

The people who use the ambulance to get aspirin are probably great at filling out paperwork. They know how to play the system.

I had a client who is paralyzed from the neck down. Filling out a form is an ordeal for him.

If you make everyone re-apply for benefits, you will keep the ambulance riders and cut off my friend.

If we can get rid of the waste in the Medicaid system, we won't have to cut off those who need it.

I saw a Kentucky study that said that there were 49 people that each went to the emergency room more than 50 times last year. No one needs to go to the emergency room fifty times in one year.

They probably weren't looking for aspirin; they were looking for the good stuff.

We need the same solution for these leeches that we have for career criminals. Three strikes and you are out.

If you go the emergency room three times in a year and don't have a real emergency, you get cut off from Medicaid.

Forever.

People can screw up and go when they should not. I did. I once thought I was having a heart attack when in actuality it was indigestion from too many meatballs at lunch. I felt like an idiot.

People can make one or two mistakes. They just can't make 50 of them.

We need to preserve the system for people who really need it.

Pills are not going to cure the ills of those wanting to rip off the system.

Especially when the pills cost $2000 per visit.

Freedom for Judges

"Freedom's just another word for nothing left to lose."
- Kris Kristofferson (Janis Joplin)

Until recently, judicial candidates could not express positions on issues. Judicial campaigns were polite affairs with each side trying to boost name recognition and a positive image.

Now campaigns can look more like professional wrestling matches. Judicial candidates have the freedom to say or do anything to get elected.The decision to run for judicial election could be seen as the mid-life crisis cure for attorneys. Any lawyer who is tired of practicing law has an odds-on shot to become a judge. All they have to do is promise interest groups that they will rule in their favor every time.

Since the election policy changed, Judicial races can be decided on social issues like abortion, gay marriage, and prayer in school rather than the candidates' ability to uphold the law. Plus, the doorway is now open for rigid ideological groups to make sure judges toe the line.

Normally, I defend the right to free speech at all costs. I am zealous about the First Amendment, but I am not sure that "free speech" in judicial campaigns is a good idea.

Judges are supposed to be impartial and look at the facts of a case. How can they do this if they take positions on issues during a political campaign before any cases are heard?

Politics are not supposed to be in the judicial system. Thus, that is the reason why judges are not elected through political parties.

I would hate to see judges running nasty campaigns against each other, especially if candidates were maliciously implying that one was crazy and another were gay.In other words, I would hate to see judicial elections stoop to the level of races for the United States Senate.

Now that the genie is out of the bottle, everyone needs to play by the new rules.

I saw where Common Cause put out a high-minded call for judges to sign "a pledge not to pledge," agreeing not to sign any pledge, promise, or commitment.

There is only one kind of judge that would sign that pledge—one that secretly wanted to lose his or her seat.

If one candidate were to sign the pledge and the other did not, the non-signer would have a tremendous advantage. Even if both were to sign, one of the sides could break during the campaign.

It would be like watching a professional wrestling match where one wrestler agrees to follow the rules, and the other brings a sledgehammer into the ring.

My bet would be on the guy with the sledgehammer.

We saw a taste of the unequal playing field in the 2004 Supreme Court race. Justice Janet Stumbo ran the kind of respectable campaign that justices for the Supreme Court had run in the past.

Her opponent Will Scott criticized Stumbo's decisions. In commercials that reminded me of the Willie Horton ads, Scott hammered on Stumbo while Stumbo avoided discussion of issues.

Will Scott is now Justice Will Scott. Stumbo is practicing law.

There are several ways for judges to protect themselves during campaigns. One is to raise money and campaign hard in the years prior to an election. Many judges are not aggressive campaigners but will have to be in the future.

The second is to go after opponents who suck up to interest groups. The public wants judges to act like judges and not sell out to groups with defined agendas.

If a well-funded judge can run an aggressive campaign just like legislators and members of Congress do, incumbents should be able to stay in office. They will need to adapt their campaign tactics to the changing times.

Like Kris and Janis said, "Freedom is just another word for nothing left to lose." Candidates for judge have nothing to lose. If they were to simply tell the right groups what they wanted to hear, they could wind up wearing a robe and sitting on the bench.

However, if we are not careful, freedom to speak may cause our justice system to lose a lot.

Sports Betting Instead of Casinos

"Every gambler knows the secret to surviving is knowing what to throw away and knowing what to keep."
- **"The Gambler" by Kenny Rogers**

I regret that we did not have someone sing "The Gambler" at my father's funeral in 1993. Dad started working in a bookmaking operation when he was only 15 years old and gambled until the day he died. He was very good at what he did.

During my father's era, almost all gambling took place behind closed doors. State lotteries did not exist, and casinos were only found in Las Vegas. The popular forms of gambling were sports betting, horse racing, and card games.

Bookmakers like Dad were small business entrepreneurs. They could not advertise or sue non-paying clients but still made a good living. Gambling allowed my parents to move from an extremely poor neighborhood to a nice one. It put food on our family's table.

While 48 states have some form of legalized gambling, only Nevada has legalized sports betting services. States that make gambling legal seem to focus on lotteries, slot machines, and casinos. This mindset is disturbing for two reasons.

Lotteries and slot machines are terrible bets, and only large corporations can own a casino. Talented people can work for a casino, but there is not a chance for those people to own one.

Instead of starting lotteries and attempting to lure big casinos, states like Kentucky should license small gambling operations like the one my father had.

Dad was able to make money in the days before ESPN and the explosion of televised sports. Millions of people participate in college basketball office pools, and there are newer sports, like NASCAR, keeping bookmakers busy. Thousands of people bet with illegal bookmakers every week, and the states should be taxing that money to provide better schools and services.

Sports gambling is a fair bet. In a football game, one team is going to win, and the other will lose. It is not a trillion-to-one bet like the lottery.

I don't like having a state's tax revenues tied to the few big corporations that own casinos. If the corporation executives commit stupid or illegal acts, like those who ran Enron, then they could drag a state down with them. Licensing a variety of smaller companies would give states a wider tax base.

States can license and regulate gambling operations just like they license and regulate banks, insurance agents, and pharmacies. Thus, innovators would be able to get into the gambling business and create more opportunities for wealth in their communities.

As a betting man, my proposal is a long shot. No one is pushing sports betting, while the casino and slot machine companies are spending huge amounts of money on lobbyists and political donations. Even though illegal and offshore bookmaking is widespread, colleges and professional teams would fight against legalizing sports betting. Also, there are people who legitimately oppose gambling for moral or religious reasons.

I am opposed to the lottery because I think it exploits poor people.

The 37 states that have lotteries seem to ignore the fact that lotteries target their poorer citizens. Sports betting and poker rooms are better alternatives because they are fair to both the state and the gambler.

My Dad ran a fair and honest operation where people got paid on time and were cut off before they got too deep in the red. His career caused him to break the law, but he was one of the most honorable men I have ever known.

Dad detested gamblers that preyed on people who could not afford to lose, and he hated games like the lottery that targeted those people.

Before states rush off to embrace casinos and slot machines, I hope they think about allowing small businesses to operate sports-betting operations and poker rooms.

As Kenny Rogers said, "The secret to surviving is knowing what to throw away and knowing what to keep." Sports betting might be the ace that states should keep.

This Side Of The Table

"It's a lonely, lonely road we're on
This side of paradise."
- Bryan Adams

My late father was a professional gambler. Toward the end of his life, he was active in helping at a soup kitchen in Cincinnati, which was run by the Sisters of Charity.

One day, as he was dishing out food to homeless people, my father was approached by the Sister who ran the program.

"Joe," she said, "What do you do for a living?"

"I'm a gambler," replied my father.

"Joe," she said, "This is the first time we have ever had a gambler on this side of the table."

The key to my father's success was that he was always on the house side of the table. He started in bookmaking in the glory days of Covington and Newport and moved into organizing junkets for Las Vegas casinos, when wide-open gambling faded from the Northern Kentucky scene.

He understood that if the house has the odds in its favor long enough, it will eventually win out every time. As he often noted,

"You never see them tearing down a casino because people beat them out of money."

First with lotteries, and now through video slots and casinos, governments realized that a very easy way to gain revenues is by allowing and sponsoring gambling.

The games that have been legalized, especially the lottery, bring in much of their income from those on "the wrong side of the table."

Some European countries limit access to the casinos to those who prove they have sufficient assets. . Various forms of stock and option trading, which can be considered a more elite form of gambling, require that those who invest in those instruments have the net worth to survive a loss.

In my father's era, bookmakers cut off bettors on losing streaks. Las Vegas casinos carefully monitored their customers and cut off their credit when they lost too much.

There have been few, if any moves by states and modern casinos to monitor the losing of their customers.

Legalized casinos, which have several games of skill and reasonable probability, gear most of their operations toward the highly profitable slot machines and video games.

Lotteries have evolved from a form of gaming called "numbers," which were formerly very popular in poor urban neighborhoods. If you go into a grocery or liquor store in any poor neighborhood today, you will see people who can't afford to lose even a few dollars standing around playing scratch-off lottery games until all of their money is gone.

I rarely, if ever gamble. I can't stand to part with my money on something that is such a bad bet.

My few trips to casinos have been bad experiences for the house. I bet very little, and I am a terror at the low-price buffet. I play high-probability games and won't go near a slot machine. I have a certain profit margin in mind and leave the second that I hit it. In short, I am a person casinos do not want to attract.

Making gambling illegal was an attempt to protect people from themselves.

It did not stop the tide but pushed it underground. Gambling for rich people, such as options trading and sophisticated stock market games, have always been allowed.

When I passed the stockbroker's test many years ago, I called my father and asked, "Why is futures trading legal but betting on the Bengals illegal?" There is no logical answer.

States like Kentucky are under a lot of pressure to legalize casinos and slot machines, and just like the lottery, they eventually will be.

When casinos opened in nearby states, they started taking revenue from Kentucky's racetracks and other forms of entertainment. Casinos understand their customers, and some of the greatest marketers in the world have been introducing many new people to their games.

Kentucky will not be able to resist the large opportunities for revenues that will exist.

When legislators do expand legal gambling in Kentucky, someone must think about and speak out for the person on "the wrong side of the table."

When I was growing up, my father would go around to the sleeping-room hotels and give out bottles of low-cost champagne at Christmas. Just like those in line at the soup kitchen, many of those men were gamblers, and the bottle was often the only gift they got.

Legalized state gambling is not responsible for most of the people who are in that position in life, but the state needs to take extreme care that it does not keep them there.

Taming the Lottery Tiger

"I've got a tiger by the tail, it's plain to see.
I won't be much when you get through with me."
- Buck Owens

When Buck Owens died, tributes were made to his great skill as a musician. Few knew that Buck was also a disciplined businessman. He owned television and radio stations and was a sharp investor.

I doubt Buck ever stood in line to buy lottery tickets.

For many people, playing the lottery is like having a tiger by the tail. It can be the worst thing that ever happens to both lottery winners and lottery losers.

I hate the lottery. I hate the big Powerball jackpots with a zillion-to-one odds. I hate watching winners completely screw up their lives like Powerball winner Jack Whitaker did.

I hate standing in line watching people buy instant-winner tickets. There is a thrill to instant-winners that absolutely escapes me.

I can see spending a dollar on a chance to become super rich. I can't see the attraction in winning two dollars and then giving it back to the clerk to buy two more dollars' worth of tickets.

Especially when I am waiting in line behind them.

I hate watching people be exploited by those who run lotteries. People go on television with an oversized check and expose their lives to the public. I hate the media making celebrities out of people who happened to pick a lucky number.

The winners aren't role models. They were just lucky. Every time someone wins a lottery, the media should black out the faces of the winners and run a story about someone who built their own business.

Or someone who helped to make the world better.

It would be better for society and better for the lottery winners too.

Building a business takes hard work and talent. Even inheriting wealth requires good genetics.

Lottery winners receive their money suddenly and are thrown into a media circus.

I hate the inane television interviews that lottery winners give. The winners always have reasonable sounding goals, like paying off their mortgage or educating their children. They never mention booze or strip joints.

They might be serious about doing something good with their money. It is just that temptation, greedy friends, and bad advice get in the way.

When you get financial planning advice from bartenders and strippers, things can get lost in translation.

I've suggested that lottery winners not take all the money in a lump sum and not tell anyone they won.

The lottery organizers came up with a game I almost like. It is called "Win for Life." It just started in Kentucky but has been played in other states.

In "Win for Life," the winner gets $1000 a week ($52,000 a year) for the rest of their life. They are guaranteed a $1 million payout.

It is the same kind of "structured settlement" concept that works for helping injured people.

Giving someone $1000 a week will improve their lifestyle but will not cause freeloaders and hucksters to knock down their door. If a person blows $1000, they get another $1000 the next week and have the rest of their lives to get it right.

Win for Life allows people to take the money in cash, but I hope that whoever wins is smart enough not to do that.

I liked the Win for Life idea so much that I thought about buying a ticket. Then I looked at the odds.

The odds of actually "winning for life" are 5,200,000 to one.

I will hang on to my dollar.

Although I love the concept, I suspect that Win for Life will not be successful. Lottery players either want the big money like the Powerball or want the immediate gratification of playing the instant games.

People playing lotteries are not really interested in a good financial planning tool. They are hooked on the gambling experience and dreams of easy money.

Lotteries are many people's "tiger by the tail."

Auto Workers Coming Home

"I come from down in the valley, where mister when you're young
They bring you up to do, what your daddy done."
- Bruce Springsteen ("The River")

My parent's generation was the last to see a multitude of high-paying factory jobs. My childhood neighbors worked on assembly lines and made good money.

Some of their children are doing the same thing

I worry about factory workers who are my age. In the unlikely event that they make it to retirement without a layoff, they won't get the pension plans their parents received and probably won't have lifetime health insurance.

The game is changing, but I don't think my old neighbors realize it. They may have to change their lives radically.

When Ford Motors announced this week that they were going to eliminate up to 30,000 jobs and 14 factories, it meant that the three big American car companies had eliminated or announced plans to eliminate 140,000 jobs since the year 2000.

Those weren't minimum-wage jobs. The jobs were the pick of the litter for blue-collar employment. Automobile manufacturers offer high wages and good benefits. They attract the best working-class employees.

Though they may work hard, there is no future for these employees at the American automotive plants. The plants in big cities are being closed one by one.

It is time for those workers to think about moving to small towns.

The exodus used to be from Appalachia to bigger cities. Songs like Bobby Bare's "Detroit City" chronicled the loneliness of small-town workers who came to big cities to get a good job.

Those people moved to big cities out of economic necessity. Many have spent their lives in places like Detroit but long for the sense of family and belonging that small communities offer.

Some of my friends and family moved to Detroit over 40 years ago. Despite all the years in Michigan, they still consider themselves Kentuckians, and Kentucky is the place that they call home.

It is time for them to return to their roots. It is also the time for small communities to roll out the welcome mat and encourage them.

The people leaving the auto industry have a lot to offer. They were making good money and hopefully saved some of it. With the lower cost of living, the displaced auto workers would be upper-middle-class citizens in any small town.

They would also have skills that could boost small-town economies.

Many government entities use tax breaks and economic incentives to attract big companies to a community.

Instead of putting the focus on recruiting big corporations, who may shut down and move to Mexico, a better use of the money would be to recruit a trained and willing work force.

Like people who have been laid off from automotive plants.

With a well-trained workforce available, small and mid-sized employers might become interested in re-locating to small towns.

It is the opposite of 'economic-development-officer-think', but it could work.

It has been tried in a less formal manner. Media icon Al Smith told me recently that a bunch of unemployed steel workers moved to London, Kentucky in the early 1980's to find work. They called themselves the "Over-the-Hill Gang" and collected their pensions while they did other work in town.

The city officials in London did not recruit them but benefited from having them.

It's time for other small towns to do the same. It is a win-win situation for all.

The changes in the world economy are making it impossible for someone to be brought up in big cities to do what their daddy did.

In a progressive small town, the children of displaced auto workers might find opportunity and growth.

Unbridled Chance at Re-Election

"The beat goes on. The beat goes on.
La de da de de, la de da de da."
-Congressman Sonny Bono

The prevailing wisdom is that Governor Fletcher should drop his
bid for reelection and do something else with his life.

Admittedly, Governor Fletcher is having a difficult time but
Fletcher is a known quantity. The people thinking about running
against him are not. It's unlikely his distant past will come back
and bite him.

Of course, his recent history has not been a bed of roses.

Some of the Democrats like Chandler and Mongardo have
been through the campaign meat grinder but none of Fletcher's
potential Republican opponents have had an intense, statewide,
vetting.

Candidates for minor constitutional offices, the state legislature, or
even congress, do not go under the microscope the way someone
running for governor does.

Before running Fletcher out of town on a rail, Republicans might
think back to 1991.

In 1991, Congressman Larry Hopkins was the choice of the Republican establishment and looked like he had a really good chance to be Governor.

Larry Forgy, (yes, THAT, Larry Forgy) challenged Hopkins for the Republican nomination. Forgy narrowly lost, 51% to 49%, even though Hopkins outspent him four to one.

Although the defeat started a string of Forgy's political losses, from Governor, to Supreme Court and recently the Republican Party central committee, 1991 was Forgy's finest hour. Forgy was able to position himself as the outsider taking on the establishment.

Even more importantly, Forgy found serious discrepancies with Hopkins's resume concerning Hopkins education and military record. After the hard fought primary, Hopkins was sunk. His campaign stumbled into the general election where Hopkins lost by what was then the largest margin in Kentucky history.

I don't know if the people thinking about running for Governor have any skeletons in their closet. They may not. If they have ever lied about anything, have a backstreet lover, cheated on their taxes, been involved in any unusual business activities, or have friends or relatives who might embarrass them, I would recommend they confess it now or forget about running for Governor.

In a race for governor, every peccadillo is going to be analyzed, scrutinized, and made into a thirty-second television commercial. It is better to have the bad news on the table early.

Vetting candidates now will allow the Republican establishment to look at Fletcher and see if they really do want to throw him overboard. He may not look so bad after the other possibilities are put through the meat grinder.

Cincinnati Post Managing Editor Mark Neikirk nailed it perfectly when he said that Fletcher political career is very ill, not dead.

Neikirk urged Fletcher to make some bold moves, show some bi-partisanship in naming people to his cabinet, and fix the merit system once and for all.

If Fletcher does that, he might get the state to focus on the important issues facing it and raise his popularity at the same time.

There is hope that Fletcher is coming around. He was spotted singing karaoke at an event in Frankfort. When he was running for Governor, he and I both participated in a karaoke event in Richmond. Everyone enjoyed watching a Congressman sing like the rest of us. He won several people over that night.

For my karaoke, I dedicated my section of "I've Got You Babe" to Fletcher as Sonny Bono had also been a Republican congressman.

Sonny was elected because people knew him and Sonny did not take himself too seriously.

Like Sonny, Fletcher is a known quantity. If he can focus on the big issues and not take himself too seriously, the beat might go on for an unbridled second term.

La de da de de, la de da de da.

Acknowledgments

You didn't have to make it like you did.
But you did but you did
And I thank you.
-ZZ Top

Hillary Clinton titled one of her books "It Takes a Village." This book is an offshoot of my revitalized career as a newspaper columnist. Although the book and column have my name on it, my work has been the product of a village of tremendous friends, family and colleagues.

In my column-making village, I have two chiefs. They are Al Smith and Jim Todd.

Al Smith is my role model and mentor. He and his wife Martha Helen play the role in my life that my parents used to fill. Al has been an enthusiastic mentor and a wonderful friend. He gives me straightforward wisdom, and he is a man I truly admire. Martha Helen is an insightful and calming force for both Al and I. I have been blessed by their coming into my life.

Before Jim Todd became editor of the *Richmond Register*, I prayed that another paper would hire me away. Like Garth Brooks said, "Some of God's greatest gifts are unanswered prayers." Jim allows me the creative freedom to say what I want to say without censorship. Jim became editor of what was universally considered the worst daily newspaper in Kentucky, and in one year's time, it was named the best newspaper in its size category by the Kentucky Press Association.

Jim is a good friend but does not let me forget the high standards that he expects me to meet. Jim was instrumental in getting my newspaper column syndicated and in helping me get this book launched.

Before my column is submitted to the *Register* and CNHI for publication, it is edited by Jonathan Moore. Jonathan was referred to me by Al Smith, and he is a great find. His suggestions, corrections, and ideas make the column stronger, and he has completely edited this book to meet his own high standards. Before I found Jonathan, the column was edited by my former spouse Landra Lewis. Landra did an outstanding job, and her insights come through in the columns she edited. Susan DeHart has served in a variety of roles at McNay Settlement Group and DonMcNay.com, which has sometimes included editing my column. She served as a second editor on this book. Her capacity for hard work is endless.

There are several at the *Richmond Register* whom I need to thank. Lorie Love, Jennifer Kustes-Thornsberry, and Jodi Whitaker have served as Assistant Editor at the *Register* and have had the responsibility of editing and placing my column. All three have been wonderful friends and colleagues.

Jodi was the catalyst for my re-launching my writing career. I cannot ever stop thanking her. I hope she likes one of my future books since she is probably not crazy about this one. I give Governor Fletcher points for recognizing her talents, personality, and capacity for hard work.

Special thanks go to Nancy Taggart, whose award-winning photography appears on the cover of this book. Nancy has won so many Kentucky Press Association awards that she needs a special room to keep them all in. I also want to thank Nick Lewis for his progressive and innovative role as the *Register's* Publisher. Joice Biazoto, Bill Robinson, and Tinsley Carter are wonderful colleagues and friends. Ronnie Ellis, at the CNHI News Service, is an incredible source of information and the hardest working journalist in Kentucky. I also need to thank Brad Dennison, Vice President at CNHI, for syndicating my column and for his help in launching this book.

Special mention needs to go to the journalists who have appeared with me on *Comment on Kentucky* and to the show's co-producer Renee Shaw. Al Cross is a frequent guest and a mentor whom I truly admire. Al, a former president of the Society of Professional Journalists, is a journalist's journalist. We all want to be like him. Ken Kurtz, Mark Hebert, Jack Brammer, John David Dyche, Barry Peel, Greg Stotelmyer, Lowell Reece, Stephanie Steitzer, Cheryl Truman, Jamie Lucke, Jim Jordan, Jamie Butters, Dick Wilson, Tom Eblen, Ryan Alassi, Bill Bryant, David Hawpe, Jim Gaines, Linda Blackford, Danielle Morgan, Tom Loftus, and Mark Neikirk have been friends, mentors, and sources of information. I also need to thank the founder of KET, Len Press, who is a great Kentuckian and a constant source of encouragement.

I'm on the radio each week on WLAP-AM (630 on your AM dial in Lexington) with Tom Leach and Tad Murray. As voice of the University of Kentucky Wildcats, Tom is one of Kentucky's best known broadcasters, yet he is also one of the most down to earth people you will ever meet. He checked his ego long before he left his hometown of Paris. Tad is a great radio veteran, and we have a lot of fun talking about my column each week. Dave Baker had me on his show several times when he was at WLAP-AM, and I appreciate it. I especially need to thank Keith Yarber, who was General Manager at WKQQ-FM in Lexington when I gave rock and roll financial advice in the early 1980's. He moved on be General Manager of all the Clear Channel stations in Central Kentucky (which includes WLAP) when I reappeared in journalism 20 years later. Keith now runs my column on his highly successful www.topsinlex.com

Byron Crawford at the *Courier-Journal* is a tremendous mentor. Byron has written two columns about my column--the ultimate form of columnist flattery. Byron was a disk jockey at the legendary WAKY rock and roll radio station in Louisville and a source for song ideas. He is also a great source of advice and a good friend.

Joe Nocera at *The New York Times* is also not afraid to tell me what he likes and dislikes. When one of the most acclaimed business journalists in history weighs in, I definitely listen. Two books Joe has authored or been involved with, *A Piece of the Action* and *The Smartest Guys in the Room*, are two of the greatest business books ever written. Joe does not normally wear white shirts but wore one once on CNBC in my honor. A big moment in my life.

I wrote that Wendell Wilson is 'the Bill Gates of Kentucky.' If you check out DonMcNay.com or UnbridledErnieFletcher.com, you can see why. I don't make a technological move without Wendell, and he is also the genesis of several of my better columns.

I'm blessed with tremendous friends, who give me column ideas, songs, and feedback.

My college roommate and lifelong friend Mike Behler edited my columns in college and then later when I wrote for the *Lexington Herald-Leader*. He remains one of my primary sounding boards, and it would be hard to imagine a better or more loyal friend.

Special mention also needs to go to Suzette Martinez Standring, Bob Babbage, Shirley Sanders, Peter Perlman, Pierce Hamblin, Jeff Chasen, Alan Stein, Samantha Bennett, Rob Dollar, Carroll and Janice Crouch, Dr. Phillip and Nancy Hoffman, Scott "Babydaddy" Hoffman, the Scissor Sisters, Paul Blanchard, Libby Fraas, Richard Vance, Sara Zeigler, Allen Blevins, John Eckberg,

Gary Hillerich, Randy Jewell, Jacquelyn Collier, Whitney Greer, Mike Tucker, Kevin Osbourn, Vicki Prichard, Tom Sweeney, Sam Davies, J.T. Gilbert, John Dicker, Harry Moberly, Carl Kremer, Donna Davis, Jim Vanover, Larry Doker, Bob Sanders, Phil Taliaferro, Melissa Davis, Bill and Jane Clouse, Gail Buck, Kathy Stein, Bill Cox, Joe Greathouse, Chuck Adams, Tom Herren, Scott Sloan, Chris Bogie, Steve Horner, Stan Billingsley, Lewis Paisley, Ivan "Buzz" Beltz, Rick Robinson, Wes Browne, Joni Jenkins, Sheila Holdt, Debbie Fickett-Wilbar, Nancy Oeswein, Lee Gentry, David Grise, Bill Garmer, Jane Prendergast, Jim Lee, Chester Finn Jr., Dennis Pike, Mike Minor, Steve O'Brien, Karen Chrisman, Maria Sanders, Richard Hay, Robb Jones, and my colleague at McNay Settlement Group, Matt Harville. They offer me feedback, advice, friendship, lyrics, and story ideas.

I need to mention my fellow members of the "Don's Get-Fit" Guys in Richmond: Clay Bigler, David Grandgeorge, Gail King, Nick McNay and Lou Romanski. If we all keep losing weight, my next book is going to be about them.

I've made it a practice not to mention living family members in my column, but they are mentioned by first name in the dedication of the book. The column would not be possible without them, and I love them dearly.

Clay and Gena are the chief officers at McNay Settlement Group and their talents and financial skills gave me the opportunity to take a mid life journey into journalism and know that my clients have the highest level of service.

I do have to give a special thanks to my daughters Gena and Angela. They gave life to the "Unbridled Penguin" logo, which has haunted Governor Fletcher since its inception. The column that their artistry inspired won the Best Columnist Award for me from the Kentucky Press Association, and became the jumping point for many columns since then.

www.
DonMcNay
.com

Don McNay: Award Winning, Syndicated Columnist

Don McNay is a syndicated columnist who views life with a rock and roll attitude. His columns are a combination of social commentary, business advice and insights on popular culture.

Don's columns appear in the Richmond (Kentucky) Register and syndicated to over 200 cities through the CNHI News Service. He has also written for Trial Magazine, National Underwriter, Claims Magazine, Probe, Trial Diplomacy Journal and numerous business and legal publications.

Don received a First Place award in the Best Column category at the 2006 Kentucky Press Association annual convention.

Don made a mid life journey back to journalism. He was one of the first Community Columnists for the Lexington Herald in 1983 to 1985 and did business commentary on WKQQ-FM radio. He also appeared on KET's longest running public affairs program, Comment on Kentucky.

For the next 20 years, McNay became one of the world's most successful structured settlement consultants for injury victims and lottery winners. He has been named to the Million Dollar Round Table for 20 consecutive years and to the Top of the Million Dollar Round Table seven times. He has spoken to over 100 legal and financial groups around the United States, Canada and Bermuda. He holds several professional designations and was a director of the National Structured Settlement Trade Association from 1998 to 2001.

In December, 2003, Don began a weekly business column in the Richmond Register and it became syndicated through the CNHI News Service in 2005. He does a weekly radio segment with Tom Leach at WLAP-AM in Lexington, Kentucky is a frequent guest on the longest running show on Kentucky Educational Television, Comment on Kentucky. McNay has appeared on numerous television and talk radio programs, including multiple appearances on WLW-AM in Cincinnati. He is on the Board of Directors of the National Society of Newspaper Columnists and serves as Editor of their newsletter.

McNay has Master's degrees from Vanderbilt University and the American College in Bryn Mawr, Pa. He is a graduate of Eastern Kentucky University and was inducted into the EKU Hall of Distinguished Alumni in 1998. He was named Outstanding Young Lexingtonian by the Lexington Jaycees in 1985. He has been named to the Top of the Million Dollar Round Table seven times and named to the Million Dollar Round Table for each of the past 20 years.

Don has been featured in Forbes Magazine, The Lexington Herald Leader, The Courier Journal, The Cincinnati Enquirer, Registered Representative Magazine and Financial Planning Magazine.

Printed in the United States
95523LV00004B/15/A